NOV 1 3

Rookie Read-About® Science

Milk to Ice Cream

by Lisa M. Herrington

Content Consultant

Dr. Rich Hartel, Professor of Food Science, University of Wisconsin

Reading Consultant

Jeanne Clidas, Ph.D.

Children's Press®
An Imprint of Scholastic Inc.
New York Toronto London Auckland Sydney
Mexico City New Delhi Hong Kong
Danbury, Connecticut

Cataloging-in-Publication Data is available from the Library of Congress

ISBN 978-0-531-24742-6 (lib. bdg.)
ISBN 978-0-531-24708-2 (pbk.)

Produced by Spooky Cheetah Press

1 2 3 4 5 6 7 8 9 10 R 22 21 20 19 18 17 16 15 14 13

Photographs © 2013: age fotostock: 11 (Javier Larrea), 15, 30 center top (Rick Mooney); Alamy Images: 19, 30 center bottom, 31 bottom (Lourens Smak), 31 center bottom (Tim Scrivener); AP Images: cover top right, 24, 27, 30 bottom, 31 top (Alan Ward/Daily Press & Argus), 12 (Don Ryan); Getty Images: cover top left, 8, 30 top (Alvis Upitis), cover bottom (Brian Leatart/FoodPix); Media Bakery: 4 (Andersen Ross), 3 top right (Jon Boyes), 28 (Kevin Dodge); PhotoEdit/Jeff Greenberg: cover top center, 23; Shutterstock, Inc.: 7 (Christopher Elwell), 3 bottom (Danny E Hooks), 3 top left (M. Unal Ozmen); The Image Works/Syracuse Newspapers/David Lassman: 16, 30 center; Thinkstock/iStockphoto: 31 center top; Visuals Unlimited/Nigel Cattlin: 20.

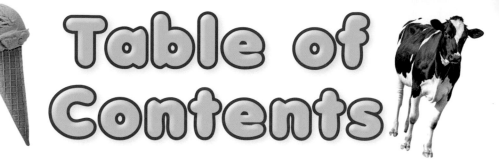

Table of Contents

4

From Farm to Factory

Ice cream is a cool treat! Get the scoop on how it is made.

Ice-cream shops offer many tasty choices.

Milk is needed to make ice cream.
Milk comes from cows.

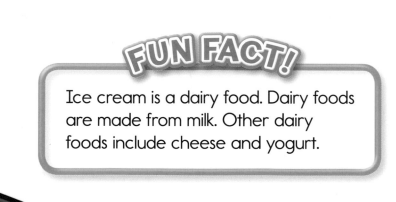

FUN FACT!

Ice cream is a dairy food. Dairy foods are made from milk. Other dairy foods include cheese and yogurt.

Farmers milk the cows. Machines pump the milk through tubes.

Farmers use machines to milk many cows at once.

The milk flows into tanks. The tanks cool the milk.

These tanks are about as cold as your refrigerator.

The milk is put into trucks.

A driver fills his truck with milk.

The trucks bring the milk to ice-cream **factories**.

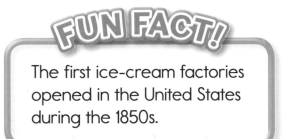

FUN FACT!

The first ice-cream factories opened in the United States during the 1850s.

16

Mixing Ice Cream

The milk goes into a big machine. Cream and sugar are mixed in with the milk.

A worker adds sugar to a vat of milk.

The milk mix travels to another machine. It is heated to kill germs. This machine is called a **pasteurizer** [PASS-chuh-rize-er].

The pasteurizer makes the milk mix safe to eat.

A Tasty Treat

The fat in the milk mix is broken up. The mix cools and becomes thicker.

Inside this machine, the mix starts to look more like soft ice cream.

The **flavor** is added to the ice cream. Then the flavored mix is put into a freezer. Air is pumped inside to keep the ice cream smooth.

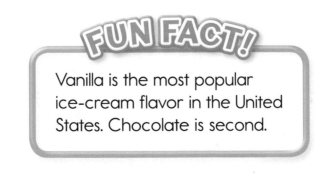

FUN FACT!

Vanilla is the most popular ice-cream flavor in the United States. Chocolate is second.

ICE CREAM FREEZER

The smooth ice cream is poured into **containers**. This is when other things, like nuts, fruit, or chocolate chips would be added.

A worker fills containers with ice cream.

The ice cream is put into big freezers. It becomes hard. Then the sweet treat is taken to stores.

A worker stacks containers of ice cream in a freezer.

Ice cream can be enjoyed in many ways. Some people like it in a bowl or a cone. How do you like your ice cream?

FUN FACT!

People in the United States eat more ice cream than people in any other country.

Making Ice Cream
Step by Step

1. Farmers milk cows.

2. The milk goes to factories.

3. Cream and sugar are added.

4. The mix goes through machines. Flavor is added.

5. The ice cream is poured into containers and frozen.

Glossary

containers (kuhn-TAYN-ers): boxes or other objects that are used to hold something

factories (FAK-tuh-rees): buildings where things are made

flavor (FLAY-vur): something added to food that gives it taste

pasteurizer (PASS-chuh-rize-er): machine that kills germs

Index

Facts for Now

Visit this Scholastic Web site for more information on how ice cream is made:
www.factsfornow.scholastic.com
Enter the keywords **Ice Cream**

About the Author

Lisa M. Herrington writes books and magazine articles for kids. She lives in Trumbull, Connecticut, with her husband and daughter. She loves hot-fudge sundaes with rainbow sprinkles on top!